I0161811

God's Armor Against
Satan's Weapons

......a spiritual battle

(Don't be caught without His armor!)

Books by Author

Travel Through Ephesians (2013)

Travel Through The Old Testament Vol 1 (2016)

Travel Through The Old Testament Vol 2 (2017)

God's Armor Against Satan's Weapons (2018)
(Tom Hiegel Bible Study Series, #1)

(Available at www.thomasLhiegel.com)

Tom Hiegel Bible Study Series: God's Armor Against Satan's Weapons
Copyright © 2018 by Thomas L. Hiegel
TLH CREATIONS, Dayton OH

All Scripture quotations, unless otherwise indicated, are taken from the NEW AMERICAN STANDARD BIBLE®, Copyright © 1960, 1962, 1963, 1968, 1971, 1972, 1973, 1975, 1977, 1995 by The Lockman Foundation. Used by permission. (www.Lockman.org)

Scripture quotations marked (AMP), "Scripture quotations taken from THE AMPLIFIED BIBLE, copyright © 1954, 1958, 1962, 1964, 1965, 1987, by The Lockman Foundation. All rights reserved. Used by permission, (www.Lockman.org)."

Scripture taken from the New King James Version® (NKJV) Copyright © 1982 by Thomas Nelson. Used by permission. All rights reserved.

Scriptures marked CEV are taken from the CONTEMPORARY ENGLISH VERSION copyright© 1995 by the American Bible Society. Used by permission.

Scriptures marked CJB taken from the COMPLETE JEWISH BIBLE, copyright© 1998 by David H. Stern. Published by Jewish New Testament Publications, Inc. Distributed by Messianic Jewish Resources Int'l. All rights reserved. Used by permission.

Scripture quotations marked HCSB have been taken from the Holman Christian Standard Bible®, Copyright © 1999, 2000, 2002, 2003, 2009 by Holman Bible Publishers. Used by permission. Holman Christian Standard Bibles®, Holman CSB®, and HCSB® are federally registered trademarks of Holman Bible Publishers.

Scriptures marked TLB are taken from THE LIVING BIBLE copyright© 1971. Used by permission of Tyndale House Publishers, Inc., Carol Stream, Illinois 60188. All rights reserved.

Scriptures marked TEV are taken from TODAY'S ENGLISH VERSION first edition copyright© 1976 American Bible Society. Used by permission.

Scripture quoted by permission. Quotations designated (NET) are from the NET Bible® copyright ©1996-2016 by Biblical Studies Press, L.L.C. http://netbible.com All rights reserved.

Scripture taken from the HOLY BIBLE, NEW INTERNATIONAL VERSION®, (NIV) Copyright © 1973, 1978, 1984 BY International Bible Society. Used by permission of Zondervan. All rights reserved.

Scripture quotations marked (NLT) are taken from the *Holy Bible* New Living Translation, copyright © 1996. Used by permission of Tyndale House Publishers, Inc., Wheaton, Illinois 60189. All rights reserved.

ISBN 978-0-9982861-2-9

Printed in the United States of America.

Contents

Foreword

This series of Bible studies is designed for both individual and small-group use and include many of the major topics of Scripture. They are appropriate for small group leaders and participants, teachers and pastors. I also would suggest the studies be utilized in colleges and universities as a reference on the topic being considered. I am convinced that nothing is more important in life, than acquiring a thorough understanding of the Bible. Therefore, this series of studies is laid out in such a way as to systematically assist an individual or a group of students, to learn the distinct unifying thoughts of Scripture. The studies are designed to be comprehensive, yet concise.

Before your group begins the first lesson, I would make the following suggestions in order to help clear the way for Bible study. Perhaps these suggestions would make an opening discussion for your group study.

1. Pray. The Words of Jesus make it clear, *"Keep asking, and it will be given to you. Keep searching, and you will find. Keep knocking, and the door will be opened to you."* Matt. 7:7-8 (HCSB). So ask Him to help in your study. The Holy Spirit is a teacher, so it would be wise to ask Him to give you understanding as each lesson is considered. Build prayer into your individual or group session.
2. Be diligent. The Words from 1 Timothy 2:15 encourage us to, *Be diligent to present yourself approved to God as a workman who does not need to be ashamed, accurately handling the word of truth.* (NASU)
3. Search. If *you seek [Wisdom] as for silver and search for skillful and godly Wisdom as for hidden treasures, Then you will understand the reverent and worshipful fear of the Lord and find the knowledge of [our omniscient] God.* (Prov. 2:4-5) AMP

This *God's Armor Against Satan's Weapons* is the first in the series of studies, and divided into twelve lessons. As a group, you may decide to expand the study into additional lessons or consolidate the suggested lessons into a smaller number. Each lesson includes **questions** to assist the student or group in understanding the topic. **Group discussion** ideas and word studies will drive the group or individual to express various thoughts. In addition, **Key Thoughts** are offered for continued encouragement.

A small group is a vital gathering for believers. It is quite personal. One week it might be a discussion on the Pastor's message, the next gathering may talk about a political topic of interest. Friends may share happenings in their individual life, or guests may have questions about Biblical issues. The small group will always make adjustments to benefit those present.

The small group leader may encourage those present to openly participate in the topic or offer a point for others to discuss. You will never be forced to speak if you are uncomfortable in doing so.

Each participant is encouraged to have his/her own Guide. An additional manual for leaders will soon be available and include many valuable materials, which will assist in the presentation of study of the topic. It is designed to benefit not only the teacher or leader of a group, but also any student desiring more depth in the study.

Lesson *1*

Spiritual Warfare Summary

Participant's Guide

1. The central verse for this topic of *God's Armor Against Satan's Weapons*, is Ephesians 6:11.

2. To study the Armor of God, we must have a clear understanding of the topic of spiritual warfare. It involves not only the wonderful armor that a believer "puts on" as a wardrobe, but also the weapons of Satan, which are used against the human race. We will include both sides of the battle in this study.

> **GROUP DISCUSSION:**
> What is the war, which we are fighting?
> Does unbelief, fear, or doubt, attack you?
> Who is the war fought with?
> How do we win.....each battle.....of the war?

3. Let's unwrap what the Bible teaches about spiritual warfare.

CLASS NOTES

Suggested books for further study on spiritual warfare:
Battlefield of the Mind, Joyce Meyer
Spiritual Warfare, Jerry Rankin
Victory over the Darkness, Neil Anderson
The Bondage Breaker, Neil Anderson
Dressed To Kill, Rick Renner
Tough Stuff, Charles Swindoll
The Screwtape Letters, C.S. Lewis

Central Verse: Eph. 6:11

NASU *Put on the full armor of God, so that you will be able to stand firm against the schemes of the devil.* **Memorize this verse.**

AMP *Put on God's whole armor [the armor of a heavy-armed soldier which God supplies], that you may be able successfully to stand up against [all] the strategies and the deceits of the devil.*

TEV *Put on all the armor that God gives you, so that you will be able to stand up against the Devil's evil tricks. (We could paraphrase here and say against the Devil's dirty tricks).*

TLB *Put on all of God's armor so that you will be able to stand safe against all strategies and tricks of Satan.*

	CLASS NOTES
KNOW THIS ABOUT THE WAR. TALK ABOUT EACH OF THESE: There really is a spiritual battlefield The battle takes place in your mind Never give up in the battle Mindsets and mentalities allow "strongholds."	

4. Before the war, in Genesis, God said everything He created thus far, was "good," "peaceful," and "war-free." ⟶

Gen. 1:18, 25
God saw that it was good.

    4.1. God made the body of a man from the earth, and He blew into the nostrils of that body His own life. He did this by saying in v. 26 *Let Us* [the Trinity] *make mankind in Our image, after Our likeness, and let them have complete authority*.......Man was the light of God's glory. All because of the words which God released, which were full of His creative power.

DISCUSS What did having "complete authority mean?"

    4.2. Concerning all of His creation, God declared in verse 31. ⟶

Gen. 1:31
God saw all that He had made, and behold, it was very good.

    4.3. Therefore in those first days, Adam and Eve were to reign as Kings and Priests to live as God's representatives on earth. There was no war or battle taking place! That is what God desired of His kingdom.

    4.4. Sadly, they made a wrong choice. Disobedience came, and the light of God's glory went out! God's plan was interrupted until, as Revelation records, His plan is completed.

4.4.1.   Adam and Eve obeyed Satan
and he, <u>legally</u>, became their overlord.
Then, there was war.

PARTICIPANT'S NOTES:

5.   Let's examine, **THE SERIOUSNESS OF THIS WAR.**

5.1. Spiritual warfare is real! It is raging today.

    5.1.1.   Not the physical battle in Afghanistan or Syria.

    5.1.2.   <u>You</u> are in <u>this</u> battle each and every day.

A KEY THOUGHT
We begin to change the outcome by changing our thoughts and words.

5.2. That is why it is important to know how to protect yourself against spiritual attacks—put on God's love-given, grace-provided ARMOR. That armor will stop every weapon of Satan, which is hurled against you.

5.3. We will look in a later lesson during this course at the battlefield. First, realize the seriousness of the battle. ⟶

Paul told us in Eph. 6:12
For our <u>struggle</u> is not against flesh and blood, but against the rulers, against the powers, against the world forces of this darkness, against the spiritual forces of wickedness in the heavenly places.

The AMP reads *For we are not <u>wrestling</u> with flesh and blood..*

5.3.1. Consider very closely, the word "*struggle*" in this verse, for this word is the key to understanding how intense and serious this spiritual warfare can become! The battle is a *struggle*.

WORD DEPTH

The root word for 'struggle' is an ancient Greek word "pale" (pal'-ay) referring to *hand-to-hand fighting in combat*. It is also the Greek word from which Palastra comes.

5.3.2. Athletes in Paul's day worked out in the Palastra, a huge building resembling a palace, dedicated to athletic skills. **Three kinds** of athletes trained for their sports: ↓

CLASS NOTES

The athlete in Rome was an important part of society. They were well known and well trained. The Romans were extremists when it came to entertainment. It is said that the Romans were interested in two things: bread and games. Athletes were a part of celebrations and funerals.

---

(1) Boxers:
The first and most feared combat sport was boxing. The boxers from the first century were not like our boxers today. This sport was so severe that few boxers ever lived to retire from their profession. Most of them died in the ring. Of all the sports, the ancients viewed boxing as the most hazardous and deadly. In this brutal and barbaric sport, the ancient boxers wore gloves ribbed with steel and spiked with nails.

(2) Wrestlers:
This was also a deadly sport in the first century. In fact, most wrestlers chose to fight to the death rather than walk out of the ring in humiliation and defeat. The sport tolerated choking and every imaginable tactic such as breaking fingers, breaking ribs by a waist lock, gashing the face, and gouging out the eyes.

(3) Pankratists:
These fighters were the fiercest, toughest, and most committed of all! No rules in this sport, they were permitted to kick, punch, bite, gouge, strike, break fingers, break legs, and to do any other horrible thing you could imagine. There was no part of the human body that was off limits.

6. **An encouragement** for each one of us, to serve as our foundation to stand on:

6.1. The real battle with Satan <u>was won</u> at a cross and the time following the cross, which included Jesus Christ rising from death and going to the Father.

    6.1.1.   The Apostle Paul made it quite clear:

    6.1.2.   Notice the word "disarmed" or "freed," it is also translated "spoiled" in the KJV.

WORD DEPTH

The word "disarmed" or "spoiled" is a Greek word, which means to strip off or to put off as one would put off his garments. This word could depict the disarming of an enemy — literally stripping his weaponry and artillery from him and leaving him without any weapons with which to respond. By using this word, the Holy Spirit tells us that when Jesus arose from the dead, He thoroughly plundered the enemy!

    6.1.3.   Then they had a party!

        6.1.3.1.   Greek writings reveal the winner of a battle would return home in celebration of victory and actually put the enemy on display; humiliating that enemy.

        6.1.3.2.   The Holy Spirit carefully tells us the enemy was stripped

CLASS NOTES

So, this first phrase in Ephesians 6:12 really carries this idea (literal translation):

"For our wrestling — that is, our intense struggle, fierce combat, contest, challenge, and ongoing conflict — is not really with flesh and blood..."

Colossians 2:15
When He had <u>disarmed</u> the rulers and authorities, He made a <u>public</u> display of them, having triumphed over them through Him.

A literal translation of Col. 2:15 could be: *"He completely stripped principalities and powers and left them utterly naked, with nothing left at their disposal with which to retaliate..."*

bare to the core, and displayed for the entire spiritual universe to see.

6.1.3.3.　　In addition, notice the word *public.* After Jesus won the battle, he displayed the triumph with a celebration. It was a party!

WORD DEPTH

The word "public" is taken from a Greek word, which is used throughout the books of the New Testament to denote boldness, confidence, openly, or something that is done blatantly or publicly.

6.1.3.4.　　A celebration of Jesus' victory commenced in heaven. it was no quiet affair! On the contrary — He boldly, openly, confidently, loudly, blatantly, and publicly exposed and displayed the enemy to the heavenly hosts! You and I may celebrate today— the spiritual battle was won.

KEY THOUGHT FOR THIS WEEK

The battle began...you and I fight with an enemy every day in one way or another. However, there is good news. Victory is assured by His armor. He has given every piece of His own armor to wear each day.

**END FIRST LESSON
NEXT WEEK'S LESSON: THE COMBATANTS OF THE WAR**

Lesson *2*

The Combatants of the War

Participant's Guide

1. In lesson one, we briefly discussed a summary of spiritual warfare. In this lesson, we discover **THE COMBATANTS OF THE WAR.**

2. You…and actually all mankind…are at war against an evil enemy, Satan. The good news is that we have been given armor to stop every weapon used against us.

GROUP DISCUSSION:
ASK the group to give their opinions on who is the enemy?

---

3. Let's review some Scripture about the **THE ENEMY.**

    3.1. First, Who Is He?

Write down your description of Satan:

_____

_____

_____

CLASS NOTES

Memorize the central verse of the Course: Eph. 6:11
Put on the full armor of God, so that you will be able to stand firm against the schemes of the devil.

Have someone read Eph. 2:2 from their personal Bible. Then read from these versions:

AMP *In which at one time you walked [habitually]. You were following the course and fashion of this world [were under the sway of the tendency of this present age], following the prince of the power of the air. [You were obedient to and under the control of] the [demon] spirit that still constantly works in the sons of disobedience [the careless, the rebellious, and the unbelieving, who go against the purposes of God].*

(from Holman Christian Standard Bible®)
And you were dead in your trespasses and sins 2 in which you previously walked according to this worldly age, according to the ruler of the atmospheric domain, the spirit now working in the disobedient.

(The NET Bible®) *And although you were dead in your transgressions and sins, 2 in which you formerly lived according to this world's present path, according to the ruler of the kingdom of the air, the ruler of the spirit that is now energizing the sons of disobedience.*

PARTICIPANT'S NOTES:

3.1.1. Paul tells us WHO is running this system of evil. He is described in Eph. 2:2 as a *prince*, a *power*. (Refer to the above translations).

3.1.2. Three things we learn about Satan in this phrase:

    3.1.2.1. #1 He's called a *"Prince."*

        3.1.2.1.1. The Pharisees called him *"The Prince of demons."* Jesus called him *"the prince of this world."*

        3.1.2.1.2. Then Paul referred to Satan as *"the god of this world."* As such he has *"blinded the minds of unbelievers"* so they can't see the truth. ⟶

    3.1.2.2. #2 He has *"power."* ⟶

        3.1.2.2.1. Jesus eternally broke this "power" of Satan. Anyone accepting Christ has this same power! ⟶

    3.1.2.3. #3 His base of power is located *"in the air."* ⟶

CLASS NOTES

Matt. 9:34
But the Pharisees said, He drives out demons through and with the help of the prince of demons. AMP

John 12:31
Now the ruler (evil genius, prince) of this world shall be cast out (expelled). AMP

2 Cor. 4:4
For the god of this world has blinded the unbelievers' minds. AMP

Power: How do you describe the power of Satan? Is this the "dynamite" power we receive as spoken of by Jesus in Acts 1?*

*The power Satan has (Eph. 2:2) is the Greek word *Exousia* (jurisdiction). The Holy Spirit gives us the "dunamis" (miraculous, mighty, Acts 1:8) or dynamite power.

When He had disarmed the rulers and authorities, He made a public display of them, having triumphed over them through Him.

"sky above"

17

GROUP DISCUSSION:
What is meant by "in the air?"

3.1.2.4.   Classical Greek used this word to refer to "the lower regions of the earth's atmosphere."

3.1.2.5.   He is not interested in controlling uninhabited places. He's the *god of this world*, where man dwells. (John 12:31).

4. Let's look at the **ARMY OF THE ENEMY.**

4.1. Colossians 2:15 notes for us that there are *rulers* and *authorities* that Jesus *disarmed.*   ⟶

When He had disarmed the rulers and authorities...having triumphed over them through Him.

4.2. The hierarchy of Satan is described in Eph. 6:12. Let's READ ABOUT THE HIERARCHY. This is important for us to clearly understand.   ⟶

In Eph. 6:12, Paul told us, For we wrestle not against flesh and blood, but against (#1) principalities, (#2) against powers,(#3) against the rulers of the darkness of this world, (#4) against spiritual wickedness in high places, (#s and underlines added for emphasis)

GROUP DISCUSSION
What does "hierarchy" mean?
Describe the "layers of command" in a workforce.
How important is each level? Does each level have individual responsibilities?
Keep this discussion in mind as we continue this lesson.

4.2.1.   There are levels of demonic powers that exist in Satan's kingdom.

4.2.1.1.   Our adversary is *real*. There are foul forces of darkness that work covertly behind most disasters and many moral failures.

18

4.2.1.2. However, these demonic spirits cannot do anything unless our mind and flesh cooperate with them!

A KEY THOUGHT
Keep your mind and flesh dominated by the Word of God.

4.3. Let's detail Ephesians 6:12.

4.3.1. Paul presents here, a divine revelation he received that describes how Satan's kingdom has been militarily aligned.

4.3.2. At the top of the list, Paul mentions "*Principalities.*" These are the most powerful demons in Satan's hierarchy. They rule and direct other groups of spiritual enemies.

4.3.2.1. We could recognize individuals who hold the highest and loftiest position of rank and authority. A Vice President or Board member.

4.3.3. A second group of evil beings is referred to as **"*Powers.*"** ⟶

4.3.3.1. Same word Jesus used in…Matt. 28:18; except the Hebrew makes it clear…ALL. *All power is given unto me in heaven and in earth.* Jesus has all power.

4.3.3.2. In Luke 4:6 the devil used this word, *And the devil said unto him, All <u>this</u> power will I give thee.*

CLASS NOTES

but against <u>principalities</u>,

Principalities: (Summarize this from our lesson)

_____

_____

_____

against <u>powers</u>

Powers: This is the same ancient word *exousia* (see page 17). Write down your thoughts on a person with jurisdiction power.

19

4.3.3.3.　　He demonstrated some of his power to Jesus, (as if He didn't know)! However, he had no ability or authority to offer "all power."

4.3.3.4.　　And **WE** were later given this identical same authority in John 1:12 *But as many as received him, to them gave he power to become the sons of God, even to them that believe on his name.*

4.3.4.　　A third tier of Satan's domain, *"the <u>rulers</u> of the darkness of this world."*

　　　　　　　⟶

4.3.4.1.　　This phrase pictures military training camps where young men were assembled, trained, and turned into a mighty army. Young soldiers being organized.

4.3.4.2.　　Think of it: This is the word Paul now uses in his description of Satan's kingdom.

ASK: What does this tell us?

A KEY THOUGHT
Satan deals with demon spirits as military troops.

4.3.5.　　Then Paul concludes his description of Satans's forces, with the bottom tier, *"spiritual wickedness in high places."* Perhaps individual or small groupings of demons spreading

against the <u>rulers of the darkness of this world,</u>

Rulers: (Whom could you call a ruler?)

Trained?
Mighty?
Organized?

against spiritual <u>wickedness in high places</u>

Wickedness: (Describe this in your own words).

wickedness in cities. Perhaps even ruling a section of, or an entire city.

> **Discuss** your thoughts about Satan's hierarchy. Offer examples of how each of these four tiers could exist.

KEY THOUGHT FOR THIS WEEK
There is no room for slackness in the life of a Christian soldier, a member of the troop of God.

AN ENCOURAGEMENT FOR EACH OF US
Always remember, every believer has far more authority and power than the devil and his forces. You and I have the Greater One living within us! That Greater One met all of these enemies described, defeating them face-to-face on the enemy's battlefield, and made an open show of that victory.

PARTICIPANT'S NOTES:

CLASS NOTES

Principalities

Powers

Rulers of darkness

Spiritual wickedness

The enemy in every battle is well-organized and has one goal in mind: Kill, steal, and destroy.

PARTICIPANT'S NOTES:

Lesson 3

Where Is This War Fought?

Participant's Guide

1. Where is this war fought? It is not kept a secret.

   1.1. The enemy does not determine the battlefield. It has been established in every human being.

   1.2. YOU determine **to win** on the battlefield.

2. Spiritual warfare in the New Testament.

   2.1. Only five times does the words "war" or "warfare" occur in the New Testament.

   2.2. Let's quickly look at those 5 verses:

      2.2.1.   2 Corinthians 10:3-5

         2.2.1.1.   Here, both "war" and "warfare" are used to refer to <u>mental bondages</u> that you must pull down.

2 Corinthians 10:3-5 *For though we walk in the flesh, we do not <u>war</u> according to the flesh, 4 for the weapons of our <u>warfare</u> are not of the flesh, but divinely powerful for the destruction of fortresses. 5 We are destroying speculations and every lofty thing raised up against the knowledge of God, and we are taking every thought captive to the obedience of Christ…*

2.2.2.   1 Timothy 1:18 ———→

    2.2.2.1.   Timothy was to remember the prophecies that had been spoken over him, that <u>by them</u> he might "wage the good warfare."

2.2.3.   2 Timothy 2:4 ———→

    2.2.3.1.   Timothy is to keep his life clear of clutter, to be <u>single-minded</u> and stay committed to the call of God regardless of the cost.

2.2.4.   James 4:1 ———→

    2.2.4.1.   This time the wars and fights described show us the real battle is with the flesh. The devil uses the mind and flesh.

2.2.5.   1 Peter 2:11 ———→

    2.2.5.1.   Here also, Peter uses war to describe the fleshly pleasures or lusts that attempt to conquer and subdue the mind.

2.3. In light of the five references in the New Testament, we can establish doctrine or teaching on the location of spiritual war. Every reference to our enemy and spiritual warfare in the Scriptures is in the context of victory.

    2.3.1.   *The mind is where this battle and war with Satan takes place.* It is the strategic center of the fight. Moreover, once you have this clear

---

CLASS NOTES

1 Timothy 1:18 *This charge I commit to you, son Timothy, according to the prophecies previously made concerning you, that <u>by them</u> you may <u>wage the good warfare.</u>* NKJV

2 Timothy 2:4 *No one engaged in warfare entangles himself with the affairs of this life, that he may please him who enlisted him as a soldier.* NKJV

James 4:1 *Where do wars and fights come from among you? Do they not come from your desires for pleasure that war in your members?* NKJV

1 Peter 2:11 *Beloved, I urge you as aliens and strangers to abstain from fleshly lusts which wage war against the soul.*

SEE the suggested books that expand this topic (page nine).

SEE chapters eight and nine **The Weapons of Satan.**

understanding, you will have less and less trouble with him. It starts in the mind with thoughts, which originate through the senses.

WORD DEPTH
Interesting to note, that the word *devil* means "one who beats against another again and again and again until he finds a foot hold, in order to establish a strong-hold." ——————➤

2.4. The teaching, which determined the location of the battlefield, is solidly established by Scripture. A short study on the mind:

   2.4.1.   By nature, the condition of the mind is hostile toward God.

Read each of the following Scriptures, allowing comments on each one. Each is printed for convenience. ——————➤

       2.4.1.1.   Rom. 8:6-7

       2.4.1.2.   Col. 1:21

       2.4.1.3.   Ephesians 4:17-18

       2.4.1.4.   2 Corinthians 4:4

       2.4.1.5.   Rom. 1:28

       2.4.1.6.   The mind must be renewed to this truth.

   2.4.2.   Even after you become a Child of God, the scriptures are clear on this subject.

CLASS NOTES

Locate a Scripture for each of these:

Devil…stirs up lies.
Satan…opposes God's plan.
Lucifer…shining one, will appear as an attraction.
Beelzebub…god of filth.
Tempter…enticer.
Prince of this world…crafts entire school of thought to seen right.
Accuser of the brethren…will condemn you.

Rom. 8:6-7 *Now the mind of the flesh [which is sense and reason without the Holy Spirit] is death. But the mind of the [Holy] Spirit is life and peace. 7 [That is] because the mind of the flesh [with its carnal thoughts and purposes] is hostile to God.* AMP

Col. 1:21 *And although you at one time were estranged and alienated from Him and were of hostile attitude of mind in your wicked activities.* AMP

Ephesians 4:17-18 *So this I say and solemnly testify in [the name of] the Lord, that you must no longer live as the heathen do in their perverseness [in the folly, vanity, and emptiness of their souls and the futility] of their minds. 18 Their moral understanding is darkened and their reasoning is beclouded. [They are] alienated from the life of God [with no share in it; this is] because of the ignorance (the want of knowledge) that is deep-seated in them.* AMP

25

2 Corinthians 4:4 *For the god of this world has blinded the unbelievers' minds.* AMP

Rom. 1:28 *And so, since they did not see fit to acknowledge God or approve of Him or consider Him worth the knowing, God gave them over to a base and condemned mind.* AMP

Scriptures to Help in Daily Spiritual Combat	
Eph. 4:23	*And be constantly renewed in the spirit of your mind [having a fresh mental and spiritual attitude].* AMP
Eph. 4:24	*And put on the new nature created in God's image, [Godlike] in true righteousness and holiness.* AMP
Col. 3:10	Colossians 3:10 *And have clothed yourselves with the new [spiritual self], which is [ever in the process of being] renewed and remolded into [fuller and more perfect knowledge upon] knowledge after the image of Him Who created it.* AMP
Col. 3:16	*Let the word of Christ have its home [in your hearts and minds] and dwell in you in [all its] richness, as you teach and admonish and train one another in all insight and intelligence and wisdom.* AMP
1 Peter 1:13	*So brace up your minds; be sober (be alert).* AMP

2.4.3.   Tighten up every area of your mind—which requires a life of commitment. <u>Day-by-day-by-day-by-day.</u>

3. Be aware of Two Kinds of Strongholds.

ASK: How do you describe a strong-hold?

3.1. The two kinds of strong holds are *Rational* and *Irrational*.

3.1.1.   The <u>rational</u> strong is a hold in your mind which usually makes sense!

⟶

3.1.1.1.   The word *reasonings* in 2 Cor. 10 :5 is taken from the

(Read this verse in several versions)
2 Corinthians 10:5
[Inasmuch as we] refute arguments and theories and <u>reasonings</u> and every proud and lofty thing that sets itself up against the knowledge of God; and we lead every thought and purpose away captive into the obedience of Christ. AMP

ancient word "logismos," which is where we get the word "logic," as in "logical thinking."

3.1.1.2.   A logical thinker many times will allow the particular thought to override faith. Every *high thing*, every *argument* which comes against His Word, attempts to establish a stronghold on the battlefield.   ⟶

3.1.1.3.   Your logical mind will try to talk you out of obeying God.

3.1.2.   Then the Second kind of stronghold is *irrational strongholds*.

3.1.2.1.   Unrealistic fears and worries.

3.1.2.2.   These are strong holds in the mind, emotions, and imagination, which you must deal with straightforwardly with the Word of God. The most dangerous time for any army is when they think the enemy is not near. Our enemy is always near, looking for a weakness to attack.   ⟶

A KEY THOUGHT
If you take your thoughts captive, your thoughts cannot take you captive!

GROUP DISCUSSION
What causes thoughts in the mind?
How do we 'clear the mind' of evil or sinful thoughts?

CLASS NOTES

2 Cor. 10:5-6
casting down arguments and <u>*every high thing*</u> *that exalts itself against the knowledge of God, bringing every thought into captivity to the obedience of Christ, 6 and being ready to punish all disobedience when your obedience is fulfilled. NKJV*

James 4:7
Resist the devil and he will flee from you. This Scripture says…you…resist. You would think it would say "ignore the devil and he will flee from you." NO, do not ignore him, pay attention to this truth.

27

Would you describe a sinful thought you have had?
LET'S PRAY TOGETHER ABOUT OUR THOUGHTS.

KEY THOUGHT FOR THIS WEEK
Pull down every mental or emotional strong hold in your life with the supernatural weapons of warfare such as positive thoughts. The Armor of God is put on to defeat the enemy.

PARTICIPANT'S NOTES:

END THIRD LESSON
NEXT LESSON: THE LOINBELT

Lesson 4

God's Armor: The Loinbelt

Participant's Guide

1. A Review of the First Three Lessons. What we know thus far:

   1.1. In lesson One, we noted that God created everything to be at peace. It was all very good.

   1.2. Also, Satan got involved and things turned; a serious war started that every human being, without even realizing, was on a battlefield; no longer at peace.

   1.3. In lesson Two, we looked at Satan, the attacker, the accuser, the power of the very air above us. His army is real, organized, and well trained.

   1.4. In lesson three, the location of the war; Imaginations.....reasonings....doubts.... strong holds in the mind, which lead to problems, mostly with the flesh.

CLASS NOTES

By now, I hope each of you has memorized our Key Scripture: Eph. 6:11

NASU   *Put on the full armor of God, so that you will be able to stand firm against the schemes of the devil.*

Lesson One
    God created; everything to be at peace.
Lesson Two
    Satan determined the battlefield and brought spiritual war.
Lesson Three
    Satan introduced types of war, each with fiery darts.

1.5. God planned redemption, and placed in every person a measure of faith in order to overcome the enemy on the battlefield. He gave that person His own wardrobe, or armor to wear. We can dress with each piece of armor.

1.6. Most of our lessons will concentrate on His Armor which each of us puts on. In two later lessons, The Enemy's Weapons I and II, we will look at what the enemy uses against us.

CLASS NOTES

GROUP DISCUSSION
Let's pause here, and note down what <u>you</u> have learned so far in those three lessons.

PARTICIPANT'S NOTES:

Write one or two things you have learned during the first three lessons. Share with the group. Also, any thoughts about warfare.

---

2. God's armor is called

    2.1.1.   *"the armor of light"* (Rom. 13:12)

    2.1.2.   *"armor of righteousness"* (2 Cor. 6:7)

    2.1.3.   And in our central verse it's *"the armor of God,"* It's His armor. And keep in mind it's a *full* armor. Total protection.

3. Why did Paul use Roman Armor to illustrate our Spiritual Armor? ⟶

3.1. Paul learned a lot about armor. His knowledge was progressive in understanding. Knowledge of anything is not instantaneous—it usually comes over a period of time, little by little. So it was with Paul's understanding of armor.

  3.1.1. During a ten year period, from the years 54 to 64 C.E., a basic insight about spiritual armor developed into a whole spiritual system of weapons.

  3.1.2. The Holy Spirit used Paul's familiarity with it, to give revelation concerning a warfare that every child of God would be involved with.

4. Let's look at an overview of the complete armor worn by a soldier in Paul's day. We will look at each piece of armor, piece by piece. It's the armor Paul OBSERVED as he came face to face with the soldier.

4.1. Let's read again in Ephesians to get a beginning picture of armor.

4.2. First, notice the words *"full armor"* or *"complete armor."* It refers to a Roman soldier who is fully dressed in his armor from head to toe.

CLASS NOTES

The purpose of a soldier's armor is:

_____
_____
_____
_____
_____

NOTE: C.E. is an accepted expression "common era." The traditional expression is A.D. The periods are identical.

As we proceed, notice the described Roman armor during the days of Paul.

Our key vese is Eph. 6:11 which you memorized: *Put on the full armor of God, so that you will be able to stand firm against the schemes of the devil.*

Then vv. 13-14 *Therefore put on God's complete armor, that you may be able to resist and stand your ground on the evil day, and, having done all, to stand [firmly in your place]. 14 Stand therefore [hold your ground], having tightened the belt of truth around your loins...* AMP

CLASS NOTES

4.3. The essential military hardware each soldier possessed included:

    4.3.1.   The **Loinbelt**

    4.3.2.   The **Breastplate**

    4.3.3.   The **Shoes**

    4.3.4.   The **Shield**

    4.3.5.   The **Helmet**

    4.3.6.   The **Sword**

    4.3.7.   In addition, a Roman soldier would not be caught, without his **spear**.

5. The **Loinbelt**

    5.1. Paul begins...with a belt! I guess I would have begun with a shield or maybe a sword.

        5.1.1.   But as we think about it, this is an extremely important piece of

Eph. 6:14 *Stand therefore [hold your ground], having tightened the belt of truth around your loin.* AMP

Isa. 11:5
Righteousness will be his belt and faithfulness the sash around his waist. NIV

Isa. 11:5
Righteousness and faithfulness will be a belt around His waist. (HCSB)

armor. It could be said, THE most important.

5.1.1.1.   The soldier wore loose fitting clothes, which potentially was a hazard. The belt strapped up the loose fitting material. Therefore truth or truthfulness pulls together all the loose ends.

5.1.1.2.   If we take away the belt, "the pants fall down." Also, much of the armor, which hung or rested on the belt...would fall. And you don't want that to happen during a battle.

5.1.1.3.   History tells us, the loinbelt of the soldier was the most vital part of all weaponry.

5.2. The Loinbelt of Truth is the written Word of God.

5.2.1.   God is saying... that which is in the center of man is most important **to** the man. His Word is to be the most important weapon in one's life.

5.2.2.   And it's quite interesting...the Bible is the only piece of spiritual armor (of all the seven pieces) that you can see and hold, the only piece that God allowed to be passed from the Spirit to our world.

5.2.2.1.   Paul confirms the importance of the Truth of Scripture, in 2 Tim. 3. ⟶

2 Tim. 3:15-17
from childhood you have known the sacred writings which are able to give you the wisdom that leads to salvation through faith which is in Christ Jesus. 16 All Scripture is inspired by God and profitable for teaching, for reproof, for correction, for training in righteousness; 17 so that the man of God may be adequate, equipped for every good work.

5.2.3.   As you keep the loinbelt on, and as you keep His Word around the center of your life, everything else holds together. Everything else is ready for any battle.

5.2.4.   All our being depends on this most important piece of armor, The Loinbelt of Truth.

KEY THOUGHT FOR THIS WEEK
Daily, be sure you wear His armor. Do not be caught without your clothes on!

PARTICIPANT'S NOTES:

END FOURTH LESSON
NEXT LESSON: THE BREASTPLATE

Lesson 5

God's Armor: The Breastplate

Participant's Guide

1. The **Breastplate of Righteousness** ⟶

   1.1. This is both a weapon and for protection.

   1.2. In 2 Cor. 6:7b righteousness is again referred to as a weapon, *by the weapons of righteousness for the right hand and the left.*

   1.3. We also find it in Isa. 59:17, *He put on righteousness like a breastplate.*

2. Understand what Paul had in mind when he used the Roman soldier's breastplate.

   > **ASK:** How would you describe a breastplate?

   2.1. It was beautiful. Gorgeous to see, usually made of a golden brown polished brass, and when the sun would strike it, it was blinding!

Eph. 6:14
Stand firm therefore, HAVING GIRDED YOUR LOINS WITH TRUTH, and HAVING PUT ON THE BREASTPLATE OF RIGHTEOUSNESS,

2.2. It covered the soldier's full torso. It certainly protected the heart and vital organs.

2.3. We are to know about righteousness, and put it on as surely as putting on our clothing. Righteousness is both an offensive and defensive weapon.

2.4. The Holy Spirit tells us in Ephesians 4 to *put on righteousness,* in order to protect us. Since it is His character, it is our chief protection against Satan. ⟶

3. We need to understand righteousness. Our mind must be renewed by His Word. A man's mind has been dominated by his senses since an early age. The mind must be transformed or renewed by meditation on His Word.

3.1. The church struggles with this topic. ⟶

    3.1.1.   We have to know, and then accept, that we have become the righteousness of God *in Christ.*

    3.1.2.   Paul, repeatedly in Ephesians says we are already *"in Christ."*

    3.1.3.   Righteousness is the very life and nature of God. That nature is imparted into us because of our being in Christ.

4. View the following six things that <u>righteousness restored</u> to us, because of Christ. They are restored by what Christ did:

DISCUSS EACH OF THESE SIX

CLASS NOTES

2 Corinthians 5:21 *For our sake He made Christ to be sin Who knew no sin, so that in and through Him <u>we might become the righteousness of God.</u>* AMP

Righteousness is:

_____

_____

_____

Romans 3:21-22 *But now the righteousness of God has been revealed independently and altogether apart from the Law, although actually it is attested by the Law and the Prophets, 22 Namely, the righteousness of God <u>which comes by believing with personal trust and confident reliance on Jesus Christ</u>. For there is no distinction.* AMP

See the author's <u>extensive thoughts</u> on "in Christ" in his book *Travel Through Ephesians,* available through your favorite online book store, or author's web site, www.thomasLhiegel.com

4.1. #1 We are **RESTORED TO RIGHT STANDING**

4.1.1.　A wonderful thought: To be in right standing with God! I never want to be in "wrong standing" with Him.

4.1.2.　Jesus stood in the face of storms and death with no fear of doubt. He placed you in right standing WITH Him.

4.1.3.　Read the wonderful statement to Job in 33:26, *He prays to God, and He is favorable to him, so that he sees His face with joy;* <u>*for [God] restores to him his righteousness*</u> *(his uprightness and right standing with God — with its joys).* AMP

4.1.4.　The NKJV reads *For He restores to man His righteousness.*

4.2. #2 We are **RESTORED TO FELLOWSHIP**

4.2.1.　Realize you are now born to be with Him in agreement and friendship.

4.2.2.　Jesus approached the Father in freedom. You approach the Father as an earthly son approaches his earthly loving dad.

4.3. #3 **FAITH IS RESTORED**

4.3.1.　Faith had been lost in the unsaved man.

CLASS NOTES

Right Standing could be defined as, "to stand in front of God without any sense of guild or inferiority."

Imagine, standing in front of God, maker of the universe. To know you have been made His righteousness is a glorious thought.

Say it: "*I am in right standing with God.*"

No inferiority complex. *He* was in fellowship. That is where *we are*, it is settled. Fellowship is "drinking out of the same cup."

Say it: "*I am restored to fellowship with my Father.*"

4.3.2.   But you are now saved, born again. You have faith inside you. Use your restored faith to BELIEVE. ———→

4.3.3.   Jesus knew Who He was and acted IN it. He didn't pray for faith or ask for it! Know who YOU are. Faith was restored in you the instant you believed in Christ. Realize you are the righteousness of Christ.

A KEY THOUGHT
Jesus had no sense of lack. He just walked with His Father. When he needed money, He had a fish caught. If He needed to feed a multitude, He broke a loaf of bread. Believe, then act.

DISCUSS FAITH
What is faith?
How do I use the faith that I know I have?
Jesus explained that doubt defeats faith. What does that mean?

———→

4.4. #4 WE ARE RESTORED TO PEACE

GROUP DISCUSSION
Do you usually have peace in your spirit?
Are you in peace about current decisions to be made or have made?
Let's have united prayer for peace in your life.

4.4.1.   Righteousness restores rest to your spirit. ———→

4.4.2.   Increased knowledge concerning righteousness brings an increase of

CLASS NOTES

Don't ever say words of doubt such as:
"I can't do this."
"I catch the flu every winter."
"My child will not be a success."

Turn your thinking and words around:
"I can do all things through Christ."
"I walk in the health of God."
"My child will be successful in all that is attempted."

Say it: *"Faith is restored in me. I am a believer. I can do all things through Christ."*

Hebrews 4:3
For we who have believed enter that rest.

peace. You will be satisfied and contented as you know your righteousness in Christ ⟶

4.5. #5 WE ARE RENEWED IN FREEDOM

4.5.1.   Mankind has always sought a spiritual freedom.

4.5.2.   Freedom from fear and doubt has been given to you because of your righteousness.

4.5.3.   You are free from the cravings of the flesh.

4.5.4.   No more leaning on self-understanding. You can walk in a sweet consciousness. ⟶

KEY THOUGHT (we have been having each one "say" who he is because of righteousness) A profession or confession of belief based on His Word, becomes your possession.

4.6. #6 SONSHIP IS RECEIVED

GROUP DISCUSSION
What is being a son?
We no longer have the right of a "**first** born son," We have the rights of **a** son. Equality in His eyes.

4.6.1.   As sons, we are welcome to fellowship with Him. Your place is now with Christ. You can talk with Him, heart to heart.

4.6.2.   Before there was an earth, God marked us out for the position and

CLASS NOTES
Say it: "*I have peace and live with it each day.*"

Say it: "*I stand in freedom which Christ has given to me.*"

place of sons in His Family. Think on what is said of us *For the Father himself loveth you.* John 16:27 KJV

4.7. Righteousness is expanded and made clear in the AMP translation of Ephesians 6:14. *Stand therefore [hold your ground], having tightened the belt of truth around your loins and having put on the breastplate of integrity and of moral rectitude and right standing with God.*

4.7.1. Integrity is vitally important to our walk with God. After we realize the vital place of righteousness, we take responsibility for our actions. Commitments are an absolute in our lives. No more making excuses for not keeping them.

4.7.2. The righteous will do what they tell people they are going to do, and, if for some reason they absolutely cannot, then they contact the person, give an explanation (not an excuse), and ask to be released from the commitment. We expect God to keep His promises, and He expects us to keep ours.

5. Finally, know that righteousness comes by your faith.

5.1.1. Not by *your* tears, but by *His*.

5.1.2. Allow the whisper of God in your spirit, Genesis 26:24 *Fear not, for I am with you and will favor you with blessings.* He gently assures us with Isaiah 41:10, *I will uphold you with the right hand of my righteousness.*

CLASS NOTES

Read these verses. They describe who you are.

Matt. 5:9
Blessed are the peacemakers, for they shall be called <u>sons of God</u>.

Rom. 8:14-15
For all who are being led by the Spirit of God, these are <u>sons of God.</u>

Gal. 3:26-27
For you are all sons of God through faith in Christ Jesus.

Say it: "*I am a son of God.*" Not THE Son, but I was adopted into His family and made one of His children.

40

5.1.3.   Paul says *"having put on"* and accepted righteousness by faith—that is the breastplate that gives us confidence so that not one word of condemnation will penetrate your heart.

KEY THOUGHT FOR THIS WEEK
Your knowledge about righteousness will change you forever. Never again can Satan stick a dart of condemnation in your mind or heart—YOU are wearing God's (and now yours) breastplate of righteousness!

---

6.   We conclude this lesson with a few of the many Scriptures, which establish righteousness as fact. These add to our **Key Thought for the week** (read each one as a group).

6.1. 2 Corinthians 5:21 *For our sake He made Christ to be sin Who knew no sin, so that in and through Him we might become the righteousness of God.*   AMP (I like to call this "the great exchange").

6.2. Romans 3:21-22 *But now the righteousness of God has been revealed independently and altogether apart from the Law, although actually it is attested by the Law and the Prophets, 22 Namely, the righteousness of God which comes by believing with personal trust and confident reliance on Jesus Christ. For there is no distinction…*   AMP

6.3. Isaiah 61:10 *I will greatly rejoice in the Lord, my soul will exult in my God; for He has clothed me with the garments of salvation, He has covered me with the*

CLASS NOTES

Eph. 6:14
Stand firm therefore, …HAVING PUT ON THE BREASTPLATE OF RIGHTEOUSNESS.

41

robe of righteousness, as a bridegroom decks himself with a garland, and as a bride adorns herself with her jewels. AMP

6.4. Isaiah 51:7, 8 *Listen to Me, you who know rightness and justice and right standing with God,......... fear not the reproach of men, neither be afraid nor dismayed at their reveling. 8 For [in comparison with the Lord they are so weak that things as insignificant as] the moth shall eat them up like a garment, and the worm shall eat them like wool. But My rightness and justice shall be forever, and My salvation to all generations.* AMP

6.5. Psalms 37:17 *For the arms of the wicked shall be broken, but the Lord upholds the [consistently] righteous.* AMP

CLASS NOTES

PARTICIPANT'S NOTES:

END FIFTH LESSON
NEXT LESSON: THE SHOES

Lesson 6

God's Armor: The Shoes

Eph. 6:15
and having shod YOUR FEET WITH THE PREPARATION OF THE GOSPEL OF PEACE.

Participant's Guide

1. Let's turn our attention to **The Shoes**.

    1.1. First let's understand the Roman soldier's shoes. Paul was familiar with them— guards certainly stood by him.

    1.2. The shoes were not some flimsy pair of sandals to wear on the sandy beach. A Roman soldier's shoes could be considered a weapon!

    1.3. The shoes or sandals were generally made of brass, composed of two parts.

        1.3.1.   The "greave."

        1.3.2.   The bottom sole of the shoe.

    1.4. Paul says *having shod your feet...*

Greaves
They were made of metal, shaped to wrap around the calves of a soldier's legs. They began near the knees and extended down to the feet, essential for the protection of the legs.

The Shoe Bottom
The shoe was made of heavy strips of leather or metal. The bottom included sharp, protruding spikes, two of which pointed toward the front. The spikes held the soldier in place during battle, and were used to kick an opponent.

Word Depth
The word *shod*, is a compound word meaning to *bind tightly on the bottom of the foot.*

43

1.4.1.   This pictures a shoe tied tightly around the bottom of the foot. The *entire shoe* protects the leg and allows solid footing for any battle.

GROUP DISCUSSION
Picture the shoe used as a weapon and discuss how it could be used by the soldier.
- ✓ The spikes
- ✓ Traction
- ✓ Protection of the entire leg, foot

1.5. *And having shod your feet <u>in</u> preparation*.....

   1.5.1.   The soldier stood in battle with shoes tightly tied to ensure firm footing. There could be no allowance for slipping and falling.

   1.5.2.   Once prepared with these shoes described, the soldier could be confident in his march toward the enemy.

2. Then Paul uses this wonderful word *"peace"* and connects it to the shoes. ⟶   (Eph. 6:15 above)

   2.1. Peace must have a strong grip on our life. We must tie His peace to our life, not be loosely attached. Be ready to march, ready for action. When the enemy tries to attack you with his many weapons, use the solid footing of peace to keep on marching.

   2.2. A few comments about peace

GROUP DISCUSSION
How can peace serve as a weapon?

CLASS NOTES

Isa 52:7
How lovely on the mountains
Are the feet of him who brings good news,
Who announces peace
And brings good news of happiness..

Can you attack the problem before you, with peace?

2.2.1. Col. 3:15 ⟶

Col. 3:15
Let the peace of Christ rule in your hearts.

This verse could be translated *"Let the peace of God be the umpire in the emotions or difficulties in your life."*

2.2.2. "Rule" here, is being the umpire, making the decision; not ruling by domination or force. Trust it! Learn to follow it! Let it rule in your mind.

2.2.3. It is time to allow the umpire of peace to rule over the problem in your life.

3. A final thought on shoes:

3.1. We read in Rom. 16:20 *The God of peace will soon crush Satan under your feet.* ⟶

Soon
Describes the Roman soldier marching in formation, lifting feet and stomping quickly and loudly. "Get out of our way, we are marching to victory. Get in our way and we will march over you!"

3.1.1. The word "crush" is an ancient word meaning *"to trample under the feet."* It was used to describe the trampling of grapes into wine. ⟶

Crush
It also carries the meaning: *"A snapping, breaking, and crushing of bones."*

3.1.2. This is what Paul says about your feet crushing Satan! If you are led by peace, it crushes Satan's plan into a powder, no longer distinguishable.

A KEY THOUGHT FOR THIS WEEK
The only place that rightfully belongs to the devil is the tiny area under the shoes on your feet.

END SIXTH LESSON
NEXT LESSON: THE SHIELD

PARTICIPANT'S NOTES:

Lesson 7

God's Armor: The Shield

Eph. 6:16   Most versions translate this phrase as *"above all, taking the shield of faith…"*

Participant's Guide

1. The Shield

2. A good translation for this verse is, *Lift up over all the [covering] shield of saving faith, upon which you can quench all the flaming missiles of the wicked.* Eph. 6:16 AMP

The Greek word denotes a **fixed position** (in a solid, fixed, place).

2.1. This is generally thought of as "above all the armor mentioned, give most attention to this shield." It is *thought of* as 'more important'. However, we must not interpret it in this way.

2.2. The Roman soldier's shield.

GROUP DISCUSSION
For what could a soldier's shield be used? Write a list of possible uses.
For example: Protection. Joined with other shields to form a wall, etc.

My list of how a shield could be used:

_____
_____
_____
_____
_____

Word Depth
The word shield in itself was used as in *a large stone* for closing the entrance of a cave. Eventually it was used to describe a large and oblong shield protecting every part of the soldier.

2.2.1.   There were two kinds of shields in Paul's day.

    2.2.1.1.   One was small, usually circular, used in public ceremonies and parades.

    2.2.1.2.   However, it was the second shield, which Paul had in mind. This one was wide and long in length, shaped like a door. It protected the soldier's entire body. ———▶

2.2.2.   This shield was massive, but at times could be rested on a small clip on the loinbelt (of Truth). We easily may conclude that the shield of faith works with the Word. It rests upon it. As we already discovered, it the belt slips, faith falls with it.

2.3. Paul relates a shield to faith. Faith is a force that a believer releases in order to work. It is to be lifted up, covering all. It is like a seed that you plant, it WILL start working the instant you release it, it is the Force of Faith; and it will begin to change the surroundings wherever it is planted. ———▶

KEY THOUGHT
Never dig up the seed to see if it is still working! You will stop it from growing and producing. Let it work unseen in the soil. (Hebrews 11:1).

3. The soldier's shield was covered with at least six layers of animal hide, tightly woven together. One piece of leather is tough, but imagine how tough and durable six layers of leather would be.

3.1. This shield had to be cared for every morning. If not, the leather would become

---

CLASS NOTES

The word "shield" in addition to being a large stone, is the Greek word *thureos.* Meaning *an oblong door that was wide in width and long in length.* The Roman shield was shaped like a door in a house.

Romans 12:3 Every person is born with faith.
For I say, through the grace given to me, to everyone who is among you, not to think of himself more highly than he ought to think, but to think soberly, as God has dealt to each one a measure of faith. NKJV
God has given you enough faith to cover you from head to toe.

48

stiff and breakable. The soldier would massage oil into the shield, keeping it ready for battle. If he neglected this daily application of oil, he in effect was inviting death.

KEY THOUGHT TO DISCUSS
Our faith requires a frequent anointing of the oil of the Holy Spirit. Paul says the shield is like our faith. It requires frequent attention. Without God's anointing of His Spirit, our faith becomes stiff, brittle and of little use.

3.2. The enemy used fiery darts frequently. Therefore, the shield would be soaked in water before battle. ⟶

3.2.1. Keep your faith dipped into the Water of the Word and the Spirit! It will extinguish the fiery darts of the enemy.

3.3. Paul says in Eph. 6:16 *"above all."* This is not a priority word or a place of importance—it is a location.

3.3.1. Think of this as "lift up your shield over all." ⟶

3.3.1.1. Faith is to be kept "**over**" everything and out in front in your life.

3.3.1.2. USE your faith daily.

3.4. What is that shield really for? Arm yourself with what the Word says about this. ⟶

3.4.1. Quench is a translation of the wonderful word (du-na-mus) which denotes great power, a *dunamus* power "over all" the enemy's lesser power. What we are seeing here is that when

Water
Used symbolically in John 3:5 of the Word of God or the Spirit of God. However, in 1 John 5:8, the Word and the Spirit are distinguished. Rev. 17:1 uses water as life.

Lift up over all (AMP)
Above all (NASU)
In all things (Douay-Rheims)

Paul continues "………*upon which you can quench all the flaming missiles of the wicked."*

you have this shield in place and is anointed with the Holy Spirit oil, dipped in the Water of The Word, and used above all, you are positioned to walk in power.

3.4.2.   When the power of God and faith get together, they become a shield to a believer. You become fortified and armed for war.

3.4.3.   The 'fiery darts of the enemy," were really the "bombs" of that day. They will be discussed in our next two lessons.

3.4.3.1.   These darts were very specific arrows, one of the greatest terrors of Paul's day. They actually had a combustible liquid on the arrow.

DISCUSS what may be considered a specific fiery dart in one's life. ⟶

3.4.3.2.   This represents the arrow the enemy sends toward you! A fire bomb into your home, on your job, on your way to church; fired into your emotions. When they hit, they can send your emotions into rage, anger, anxiety, worry, unbelief…on and on.

KEY THOUGHT FOR THIS WEEK
Live in His presence every day. Ask for the oil of His Spirit to renew you. Do not allow a hard brittle shield to be out in front in your battle. Do not allow your shield to get cracked.

I Peter 1:4,5 *to obtain an inheritance which is imperishable and undefiled and will not fade away, reserved in heaven for you, 5 who are protected by the power of God through faith.*

2 Sam. 22:3
my God is my rock, in whom I find protection.
He is my shield, the power that saves me,
and my place of safety.
He is my refuge, my savior,
the one who saves me from violence.
NLT

My list of fiery darts that may come against my breastplate or shield. These may be mentioned again in the next chapter.

_____
_____
_____
_____
_____

END LESSON SEVEN
NEXT LESSON: THE ENEMY'S WEAPONS I

PARTICIPANT'S NOTES:

PARTICIPANT'S NOTES:

Lesson 8

The Enemy's Weapons I

Participant's Guide

1. A key thought from the previous chapter.

   1.1. Paul wrote in Eph. 6:16 *"....you can _quench_ all the _flaming missiles_ of the wicked."* These darts were very specific arrows, one of the greatest terrors of Paul's day. They actually had a combustible liquid on the arrow.

   1.2. This represents the arrow the enemy sends toward you! A fire bomb into your home, on your job, on your way to church; fired into your emotions. When they hit, they can send your emotions into rage, anger, anxiety, worry, unbelief, etc.

2. We have an enemy. He is described in Eph. 2:2 as the _prince_ of the _power_ of the _air_.

3. Paul offers us three facts about this enemy.

   3.1. (1) Paul identifies him with the Greek word for prince, "archonta" meaning *one in a ruling position.*

Review the names of our enemy, listed on page twenty-five. Can you list any other names or designations for this enemy?

What else could be listed as a "fiery dart" hurled towards your life?

3.2. (2) He has power, the Greek word "exousia" for *authority*. This ruler of a dark world has real authority.

3.3. (3) Satan's base of power and authority is in "the air." This is the Greek word "aer" used to describe *the lower, denser regions of the earth's atmosphere.*

4. Notice how Peter describes him. ———→

1 Peter 5:8
Your adversary, the devil, prowls around <u>like</u> a roaring lion, seeking someone to devour.

4.1. This enemy would like you to envision him as a fearful *roaring lion.* However, I always note that Peter, given words by the Holy Spirit, explains it as <u>like</u> *a roaring lion.* In actuality, the believer has the armor, which sees through the disguise. Satan has no armor! In reality, to every believer, the roaring lion is a tiny pussycat.

5. Jesus made a very clear statement about the enemy in our battles. He actually compared Himself and a thief. It was perhaps the only time He gave us a quick picture of the one who is our enemy. He said this thief has <u>only one goal</u> in his existence. Let's read it… ———→

John 10:10
The thief comes <u>only</u> in order to steal and kill and destroy. <u>I came</u> that they may have and enjoy life. AMP

5.1. Notice how Jesus contrasts Himself with our enemy. Jesus is the opposite of this thief.

6. We note the reason why we are strongly instructed to put on God's armor. It is written by Paul just before our central verse. ———→

Eph. 6:10-11
Finally, be strong in the Lord and in the strength of His might. 11 Put on the full armor of God, <u>so that</u> you will be able to stand firm against the schemes of the devil.

The word "devil" comes from the Greek word *diabolos*, which means "to oppose."

6.1. We put on His armor to make a strong stand against the devil. Verse 11 identifies the fact that Satan has weapons. Notice the various words chosen by the following translators to describe Satan's body of weapons.

stand up against [all] the <u>strategies</u> and the <u>deceits</u> of the devil. (AMP)

defend yourself against the devil's <u>tricks.</u> (CEV)

6.2. Most of the attacks the devil wages against you will occur in your mind. He knows your mind is the control center for your entire life. He would like to take control over one tiny area in your mind, hoping to expand it to others areas. A small little unbelief in one area is a strong hold he will develop.

PARTICIPANT'S NOTES:

7. In the remainder of this lesson, along with next week's lesson, we will briefly mention a few of the enemy's weapons, which he hurls against all human beings, especially God's warriors. An extensive list of many additional weapons of Satan follows lesson nine. Each one could be discussed in more detail as a class. We also offer the Scriptures or *sword* to use in the victorious battle against each of the enemy's weapons.

CLASS NOTES

Eph. 6:11
stand against the tactics of the Devil. (Holman Christian Standard Bible)

stand firm against all strategies of the devil. (NLT)

stand against the deceptive tactics of the Adversary. (Complete Jewish Bible)

My list of Satan's weapons that may come against me. You may have discussed these above or in chapter 7.

➤
➤
➤
➤

7.1. WEAPONS OF SATAN. *Fear, worry, cares.*

7.1.1. Fear has no place in a believer. It may try to find a place; perhaps in your safety, work place, family, or health. However, it does not belong in you.

7.1.2. Satan uses fear, because it is a thief. It steals peace, joy, and plunders our hope.

7.1.3. Fear may also be a phobia, which most people suffer from at some point in their lives.

DISCUSS what may be considered a phobia in one's life.

7.1.4. This is one of Satan's most used and most powerful weapons. They are not "natural," or "normal." Rather the enemy strikes you with this deadly weapon.

7.1.5. Our culture conditions us to be fearful of people because they look different or act different.

7.1.6. Anxiety is a type of fear. Anxiety just lacks an object or cause. You may be anxious because of an unknown

CLASS NOTES

What are some additional words that describe "fear?"

Examples of a phobia

- Fear of enclosed places
- Fear of blood
- Fear of being alone
- Fear of disease
- Fear of animals
-
-
-
-

56

outcome of an event. Do not allow an anxious trait to persist. Many are temporary and will pass! The concern is when the anxious trait continues over a long period of time. Then you MUST use God's sword to remove it.

7.1.7. Anxiety may lead to what we would call a panic attack. These may occur with any phobia that is not defeated.

AS A CLASS, you may want to pause and discuss fear and where it leads. What are other types of fear? A time of prayer is appropriate.

7.1.8. God's Sword will defeat this weapon. When you say His Word, the enemy must be silent. Insert in these Scriptures a personal positive affirmation by inserting your name. For example, *"Tom, don't be afraid, for I am with you. Don't be afraid Tom, for I am with you."* (Isa. 41:10). Or say *"I give my burdens to the Lord, He will take care of me."* (Ps. 55:22).

7.1.9. Search out Scriptures that assure you of His deliverance. Write them down in these notes, to refer to later, when you need a sword. Make them personal!

MY LIST OF SWORDS TO USE WHEN FEAR STRIKES.

7.1.10.   See Matt. 4:1-11 for Jesus' method. Use these Scriptures when you experience any type of fear.

CLASS NOTES

THE SWORD **AGAINST FEAR**

2 Tim. 1:7
For God has not given us a spirit of fear, but of power and of love and of a sound mind. NKJV

Rom. 8:15
For you did not receive the spirit of bondage again to fear, NKJV

Neh. 4:14
Do not be afraid of the enemy; AMP

Ps. 118:6
The Lord is on my side; I will not fear. AMP

Ps. 56:4
I will not fear. AMP

7.2. WEAPONS OF SATAN *Deception, lies*

7.2.1. Satan is deceptive; he lies and distorts the truth of the Scriptures. He speaks to individuals on the battlefield of the mind-using untruth.

Anything in our mind that is contrary to the truth of Scripture is a lie from Satan.

7.2.2. He is clever and can convince us that wrong is right and right is wrong. The Scripture describes him as being *disguised* as an angel or messenger of light.

7.2.3. As a false "light," he attempts to deceive one into sinful actions and disguising them as acceptable behavior. Even a believer is sometimes fooled into criticizing others, thereby creating dissension and conflict. ——►

GROUP DISCUSSION
How does our spiritual enemy "disguise" a truth and make it look like "light?" Examples? Locate some of the many verses that say, "*Do not be deceived.*"

7.2.4. He plants unclean thoughts in our minds and makes us believe they are of no consequence since we are under grace. That is a lie from Satan's

John 8:44
Whenever he speaks a lie, he speaks from his own nature, for he is a liar and the father of lies.

2 Cor. 11:3
as the serpent deceived Eve by his craftiness, your minds will be led astray from the simplicity and purity of devotion to Christ.

2 Cor. 11:14
Satan himself masquerades as an angel of light...AMP

Rev. 13:14
he deceives those who dwell on the earth.

domain. He is deceptive; he lies and distorts the Truth. His nature is to be an adversary, placing any means of lie in front of you.

7.2.5. Many of his lies divert us from God's leading. He can cause us to waste hours and days in entertainment and activity, stealing our praise and worship time.

7.2.6. When Satan speaks to our mind, bring the thought in captivity to what Christ has told us. Because Satan's primary weapon is the lie, our defense is the Truth. Exposing a lie with the truth breaks the liar's lie. That is why Paul's first piece of armor to stand against the enemy is "the belt of Truth" which we briefly explored. It holds everything together.

7.2.7. An additional "twist" of truth by Satan is his manipulation of circumstances. He will place in your way, what appears to be a terrible or disruptive "fact." It may be what appears to be truth, but just a misunderstanding. Once the "fact" is acted upon and accepted, additional circumstances are placed before you, which add to the manipulation.

7.2.8. This grouping of misleading circumstances can lead to a personal breakdown and become a temporary depression or oppression. Paul's answer to this is stated in many of his writings. Gal. 5:1 *Christ set you free. Keep on standing firm therefore and stop being subject again to a yoke of bondage.* (Kenneth S. Wuest translation). *So take your stand! Never*

THE SWORD AGAINST DECEPTION

2 Thess. 2:3
Let no one in any way deceive you.

Eph. 5:6
Let no one deceive you.

James 1:16-17
Do not be deceived, my beloved brethren.

1 John 3:7
Little children, make sure no one deceives you.

again let anyone put a harness of
slavery on you. (from THE MESSAGE).

THE C.S. LEWIS CLASSIC, Screwtape tells of an enemy determined to defeat the Christian's walk. He wrote, "delude him, deceive him into thinking that he still has personal rights and can claim ownership of time and possessions instead of having died to self and yielded them to God." The book would be an excellent DISCUSSION during these sessions.

PARTICIPANT'S NOTES:

END EIGHTH LESSON
NEXT LESSON: THE ENEMY'S WEAPONS II

Lesson **9**

The Enemy's Weapons II

Participant's Guide

7.3. **WEAPONS OF SATAN** *Temptation*

7.3.1. This is one of Satan's most used weapons and the one we are most familiar with. The Scriptures tell us Satan is the tempter. He is behind every temptation.

7.3.2. However, Satan cannot make us do anything <u>we do not choose</u> to do.

DISCUSS by name. What could be called a temptation in one's life?

7.3.3. Keep in mind, Satan causes an attraction to things of the world, such as

CLASS NOTES

Matt. 4:3
And the <u>tempter</u> came and said...

1 Thess. 3:5
the <u>tempter</u> might have tempted you.

fleshly or carnal activities. He does tempt one to sinful behavior, actions, words, and attitudes. He persuades us to focus on ourselves, what we want, what we think we need. Selfish gratifications many times rule our minds and flesh.

7.3.4. Paul in 1 Thess. 3:5 points out that his labor in bringing many to Christ would have been in vain if they were to yield to Satan's temptation and deny their faith. ⟶

7.3.5. Satan is familiar with the nature of man. Even a believer has some of the old man remaining. Satan appeals for one remembering the old self and the enticement, which it draws. Satan begins with the same temptation he presented to Eve. "Are you sure it is not okay to partake of the fruit?"

7.3.6. **ASK:** What are the three categories of temptation mentioned by John in his first epistle, chapter 2 vv. 15-16? (see Scripture printed above).

THE SWORD AGAINST TEMPTATION

Matt. 6:13
'And do not lead us into temptation, but deliver us from evil.

Luke 22:40-41
"Pray that you may not enter into temptation."

1 Cor. 10:13
No temptation has overtaken you …and God is faithful, who will not allow you to be tempted beyond what you are able, but with the temptation will provide the way of escape also, so that you will be able to endure it.

Luke 4:6-7
The Devil said to Him, "I will give You their splendor and all this authority, because it has been given over to me, and I can give it to anyone I want…" (HCSB)

7.4. **WEAPONS OF SATAN** *Pride*

7.4.1. Satan would attempt to make one live for self. Not only does he temp with fleshly gratification, but also puffs one up with pride of self.

7.4.2. Satan's opposition to believers was evident in the temptations of Jesus. What is noticeable is that <u>Jesus did not contradict the right of Satan to</u> make that claim. When any nation, government, or people do not acknowledge Christ as Lord, Satan has dominion. He wants no one becoming a follower and servant of Christ.

7.4.3. Jesus did not yield to that real temptation of pride.

7.4.4. God will not share His glory with anyone. Never take credit for anything except that which God provides. Paul's experience recorded in 2 Cor. 12 tells of God's way of dealing with pride. God's way is a humble spirit. Open to verses 1-12 in your Bible.

7.4.4.1. Paul had a divine vision of being lifted to the third heaven, the presence of God. He was in a position that could have eventually led to "self exaltation," pride.

7.4.4.2. What did Paul say about the result? Didn't he identify Satan as a messenger of the "thorn?" God could have put a hedge of protection around Paul or just removed the attack.

THE SWORD AGAINST PRIDE

1 Cor. 13:4-5
love does not brag and is not arrogant…

Prov. 8:13
Pride and arrogance and the evil way And the perverted mouth, I hate.

Isa. 2:11
11 Human pride will be brought down. (New Living Translation)

Prov. 29:23
A man's pride will bring him low, But a humble spirit will obtain honor.

63

7.4.4.3.   However, God wanted humbleness rather than pride. He wanted Paul to end self and surrender to Him. Paul's "test" was in how he would respond, and he passed! If we humble ourselves, acknowledging our need, God gets the glory.

PARTICIPANT'S NOTES:

THE SWORD AGAINST PRIDE

1 Thess. 2:18-19
1 For we wanted to come to you — I, Paul, more than once — and yet Satan hindered us.

Rom. 15:22-23
For this reason I have often been prevented from coming to you.

7.5. WEAPONS OF SATAN: Hindrances

7.5.1. He is a Hinderer. He constantly blocks our way toward good. He opposes everything we do to glorify Christ. That is his purpose. Steal any glory that should go to God.

> **Note from the author:** When I left the full time pastoral ministry, Satan didn't strike at my salvation. That was a done deal! His intentions were to stop glory going to God from my life.

7.5.2. Every time he hinders you in doing good works, he takes glory from God. Look at what Paul said ———→

7.5.3. Hindrance is a co-worker with procrastination. Satan does many things to hinder us from doing what God wants from us. Perhaps it's some circumstance or event that hinders.

7.5.4. If Satan cannot get one to sin or yield to his weapon of temptation, he simply uses a weapon to hinder us from doing what God wants us to do. This weapon has upset the many opportunities a believer has to show another the goodness of Christ. "Things" keep us from talking with a neighbor of co-worker. Satan is a master of "little hindrances."

1 Thess. 2:18-19
1 For we wanted to come to you — I, Paul, more than once — and yet Satan hindered us.

Rom. 15:22-23
For this reason I have often been prevented from coming to you.

65

7.5.5. Hard to imagine, but many in certain "religions" are convinced they are Christians is spite of the fact that they have never been born again by trusting in Christ. A hindrance has kept them from truth. Perhaps the most prominent barrier Satan uses is hindering one from believing John 14:6. ⟶

7.5.6. Satan is the god of this world, the prince of the power of the air. He may simply use a circumstance or event to steal your time—wasting the opportunity that God has opened to you. To combat this, never fail to walk in harmony with the Spirit of God.

Key Thought
As we fellowship with God and commune with the Holy Spirit, we are at our best to hear God's direction. Let us discipline our time, set our mind on God, and do all that we can to bring Him glory through our lives.

7.6. Finally, DISCUSS the following more complete list of Satan's flaming arrows, which are used to strike against the believer's shield. Have the members of your group pick one or more to relate to. Look up a definition of each one. Discuss as many as time will allow. Taken together, they are all included in Satan's quiver of weapons, influencing one to choose self rather than God.

CLASS NOTES

Jesus said to him, "I am the way, and the truth, and the life; no one comes to the Father but through Me.

THE SWORD AGAINST HINDRANCES

Phil. 4:13-14
I can do all things through Him who strengthens me.

Col. 1:11
strengthened with all power, according to His glorious might, for the attaining of all steadfastness and patience.

Mark 11:23
whoever says to this mountain, 'Be taken up and cast into the sea,' and does not doubt in his heart, but believes that what he says is going to happen, it will be granted him.

2 Cor. 12:10
So for the sake of Christ, I am well pleased and take pleasure in infirmities, insults, hardships, persecutions, perplexities and distresses; for when I am weak [in human strength], then am I [truly] strong (able, powerful in divine strength). AMP

Abuse	Delusion	Harassment	Negativity
Accusation	Depression	Homosexuality	Pity, Abandonment
Addiction	Dissension	Indifference	Rebellion
Anger	Doubt	Insecurity	Rejection
Bitterness	Entanglements	Irritations	Resentment
Bondage	False Impressions	Jealousy, envy	Stigmatization
Complacency	Frustrations	Laziness	Suicidal thoughts
Condemnation	Gossip	Manipulation	Unforgiveness
Covetousness	Guilt	Mistrust	Unholy living

PARTICIPANT'S NOTES:

PARTICIPANT'S NOTES:

Lesson *10*

God's Armor: The Helmet

Participant's Guide

1. We continue in this session, with God's Armor.

2. The Helmet ⟶

    2.1. The Divine Warrior is described in Isa.
    59:17 *He put.......a helmet of salvation on His head*

    DISCUSS
    How is salvation like a helmet?
    Why did the Holy Spirit use this specific piece to compare it to salvation?
    How does salvation equip us for battle?

    2.2. The Helmet is a fascinating piece of armor.

    2.2.1.   The soldier's helmet was very ornate and intricate. It really looked more like a piece of artwork than a helmet. It was beautiful!

    2.2.2.   Many were covered with engravings, nature scenes, and animals. It was never considered plain, simple, or basic.

    2.2.3.   Picture it with a huge plume of bright feathers shot out the top!

CLASS NOTES

Let's review our central verse again; Eph. 6:11. Someone quote it using the version of your choice.

Put on God's whole armor [the armor of a heavy-armed soldier which God supplies], that you may be able successfully to stand up against [all] the strategies and the deceits of the devil.   AMP

Eph. 6:17 *And take the helmet of salvation*

1 Thess. 5:8
and as a helmet, the hope of salvation.

Isa. 59:17
17 He put on......a helmet of salvation on His head.

A fun exercise would be to Google "ancient helmet images" and view some examples. Someone could do this in class, for all to view. Perhaps use "ancient Roman helmets."

2.2.4.	In addition, it was very strong—nothing could pierce it. It protected the major target in battle—the head.

2.3. Some additional thoughts concerning salvation: ⟶

2.4. Salvation is God's most glorious gift. It is the <u>hope</u> of humankind. The act of <u>obtaining</u> salvation is not the concern in this passage. Satan wants to destroy the believer's assurance of salvation by using his own weapons of doubt and discouragement.

2.5. Remember what the New Testament teaches about spiritual warfare. It takes place on the battlefield of the mind. (SEE chapter Three).

2.5.1.	The head must be totally guarded and protected.

2.5.2.	The helmet fits tightly around the head. The helmet was intended to "save" a man's head.

2.5.3.	This helmet, which protects the *battlefield*, blocks the only road to your life.

2.5.4.	Satan plays mind-games with you through thoughts; it is his only method!

2.6. Consider Paul's thought in 2 Cor. 10:5: ⟶

2.6.1.	Notice, he says nothing about Satan in this verse. He does not say "and bringing the devil into captivity."

2.6.2.　　By using these words Paul tells us it won't be easy. We have to get tough and forcibly bring a thought captive. Grab hold of an emotion; put it under your authority as a believer.

3. Then let's briefly look at what generally **happens** if your fail to take your thoughts captive.　　　　　　　　　——————▶

3.1. "Oppression" is found in this verse.

　　3.1.1.　　Oppression is a powerful force that comes to dominate or manipulate.

　　3.1.2.　　It was used to describe a tyrant king who forced his will on others. Against their wishes, this king would (1) tell them what to eat (2) where they would live and (3) how much money they could make. This has always been Satan's strategy.

　　3.1.3.　　When any stronghold in your mind goes unchallenged, oppression WILL be the result.

　　3.1.4.　　Be confident that salvation, when wrapped around your brain, will protect you. No negative or satanic thought will find a place in you. It will not work because your salvation is stronger.

3.2. Here are two further thoughts to consider:　　　　　——————▶

　　3.2.1.　　**A Sound Mind** from 2 Tim. 1:7. It means "think intelligently," make sense in every thought that comes. Have a disciplined mind. Review two kinds of strongholds/thoughts from lesson three.　　——————▶

CLASS NOTES

Acts 10:38
How God anointed and consecrated Jesus of Nazareth with the [Holy] Spirit and with strength and ability and power; how He went about doing good and, in particular, <u>curing all who were harassed and oppressed by [the power of] the devil</u>, for God was with Him. AMP

2 Tim. 1:7 *For God has not given us a spirit of fear, but of power and of love and of <u>a sound mind</u>.*　NKJV

Eph. 2:12-13
12 that <u>at that time</u> you were without Christ, 13 <u>But now</u> in Christ Jesus… NKJV

3.2.2. **A Transformed Mind** from Eph. 2. It deals with how your mind WAS, → and how it IS now. So, Paul says ACT LIKE IT

4. Salvation is much more than a mind protector.

CLASS NOTES

See author's book *Travel Through Ephesians* for "before and after of salvation."

Word Depth

Salvation is an all-inclusive word, which includes deliverance, safety, peace, harmony, victory, prosperity, and health. It is the <u>rescue</u> from the danger of inherited sin nature and the <u>restoration</u> to wholeness.

4.1. Too often the word salvation is minimized and reduced to unimportance.

4.2. It is many times thought of as a free pass into heaven. A ticket punched for a ride in the skies.

4.3. Salvation, purchased by Jesus Christ, is a new realm of life having an impact on the present life. Its benefits are innumerable, some of which are noted in the above brief word study.

4.4. It is both immediate and life long. You are redeemed immediately. Then the benefits, such as protection, restoration, and healing are introduced. Each must be understood, received, and "put on."

4.5. As we close this session, read and consider together, the following Scriptures.

4.5.1. Rom. 5:9-11 ⟶

4.5.1.1. List the various thoughts included in this passage.

9 Much more then, having now been <u>justified by His blood,</u> we shall be <u>saved from the wrath of God</u> through Him. 10 For if while we were enemies we were <u>reconciled to God</u> through the death of His Son, much more, having been reconciled, we shall be <u>saved by His life</u>. 11 And not only this, but we also exult in God through our Lord Jesus Christ, through whom we have now received the reconciliation.

72

4.5.2.   James 1:21-22.

   4.5.2.1.   Note that the book of
            James was written to believers.

   4.5.2.2.   What did they have to do in
            order to grow their salvation?

   4.5.2.3.   Salvation also includes
            sanctification. Explain
            sanctification and how it is
            connected to salvation.

4.6. Now you can better understand how
     salvation is put on like a helmet.

KEY THOUGHT FOR THIS WEEK
Celebrate your new life, which you have for the rest of your days! Whatever happens this week, or next week, or the following week, be comfortable wearing the beautiful helmet which God gave to you.

PARTICIPANT'S NOTES:

END LESSON TEN
NEXT LESSON: THE SWORD

PARTICIPANT'S NOTES:

Lesson 11

God's Armor: The Sword

Participant's Guide

1. The Sword

    1.1. There were 5 distinct kinds of swords available to the Roman soldier.

    1.1.1.   The **first** was called a "gladius" sword. This one was extremely heavy, broad-shouldered with a huge blade; probably the most beautiful. Many times this sword was displayed in public ceremonies.

    1.1.2.   The **second** was very short and narrow. It was very light and easy to use.

    1.1.3.   The **third** was even shorter. We could think of it as more a dagger than a sword.

    1.1.4.   The **fourth** was a long, very slender sword, mostly used by Calvary rather than infantry. Many times, it was used for sport.

1.1.5.   And the **fifth** sword, called a **(ma-chai-ri)** sword. This was a brutal weapon nineteen inches long, razor sharp on both sides.

1.2. The Holy Spirit chose the fifth of the possible words, *machairi.*

1.2.1.   By doing this, he boldly states that God has given the Church a weapon that is useful, portable, and brutal to the enemy! As Paul explains it— *the Word of God.*

1.2.2.   This expression "*Word,*" is the Greek word *rhema.*   ⟶

Rhema describes something that is *"spoken clearly, spoken in unmistakable terms, spoken vividly, spoken in undeniable language, or spoken in unquestionable, certain, and definite terms."*

1.2.2.1.   It is the idea of a quickened word, a word from the Lord that the Holy Spirit drops into our mind.

> **ASK:** Have you ever had God "drop" into your spirit, a word to offer someone? Perhaps He had a word that came alive to you, to assist in some situation in your personal life.

1.2.2.2.   Jesus talked about this in John 14:26   *But the Comforter, the Holy Spirit, Whom the Father will send in My name [in My place], He will teach you all things. And He will cause you to recall (will remind you of, bring to your remembrance) everything I have told you.* AMP

1.2.3.   Every day we must read the written word into our spirit. Deposit the Living Word, into your life.

1.2.4.   As that is done, the Holy Spirit can drop a *rhema* into our heart or remind us of a verse. Chances are quite questionable of this if the Holy Spirit has no "word" to call to remembrance.

1.2.5.   It comes at a specific time for a specific purpose.

1.2.6.   So when Paul says the *sword that the Spirit wields, which is the Word of God,* he's referring to the Holy Spirit's ability to make a word alive in you at exactly when you need it. That's *rhema*! Actually, it is the only weapon a soldier needs in battle. His Word spoken, to you and in you, always wins.

1.2.7.   Note that the sword and loinbelt are connected closely. The sword dangled down from a clip on the left side of that belt. $\longrightarrow$

1.3. The *machairi* sword comes out of the loinbelt (truth) and becomes an empowering specific verse at the point of need. It is a specific word to deal the enemy a fatal blow in the midst of battle.

1.3.1.   The specific Word to Noah was short and direct.

1.3.2.   Abraham was called to leave everything in *three* verses! *A rhema* word.

1.3.3.   Joseph heard it in three verses of *rhema*, telling his future.

CLASS NOTES

The loin belt of truth, which we discussed previously, is the entire written word, like the larger sword. We need the *large sweeping sword* at all times.

77

1.3.4.   A short 2" penetration by the small deadly *machairi* sword is all that was required to kill. That is all the Holy Spirit needs to drop into your spirit, just the rhema you need to win.

2. A "two-edged sword."

2.1. This is really one of the oddest words in the New Testament.

2.2. The "two-edged" literally should be translated a "two-mouthed" sword!

2.3. His sword cuts two ways. It cuts twice.

2.3.1.   **One** sharpened edge came into being when originally it proceeded from the mouth of God, with all its creative power! The **second** cutting edge is added when the Word of God proceeds out of YOUR mouth! That is when it becomes a weapon. One is great, but it takes two edges to stop the enemy of your battle!

A KEY THOUGHT FOR THIS WEEK
The Word of God is the Truth concerning every area of life. Weigh every situation in the light of Word and with the barometer of Word. Draw it from your spirit as needed.

PARTICIPANT'S NOTES:

CLASS NOTES

Revelation 1:16 *and from His mouth there came forth a sharp two-edged sword.*

Revelation 2:12 *Then to the angel of the (church) in Pergamum write: These are the words of Him Who has and wields the sharp two-edged sword.*

Hebrews 4:12 *For the Word that God speaks is alive and full of power [making it active, operative, energizing, and effective]; it is sharper than any two-edged sword.*

END LESSON ELEVEN
NEXT LESSON: THE SPEAR

Lesson 12

God's Armor: The Spear

Participant's Guide

1. The Spear

    1.1. Sometimes the armor is taught as six pieces and ending with the Sword.

    1.2. However, Paul *continues* with his description of *spiritual* armor. →

        1.2.1. Most study guides or commentators agree there are indeed seven pieces of armor. This final piece generally is not illustrated by a specific piece of armor.

        1.2.2. *I suggest* it is indeed a part of armor; the piece of armor that almost every soldier carried. It is a spear or lance; some would call it a javelin.

2. For our purposes in this study, we will call this the Spear of Prayer and Supplication.

    2.1. The spear of Paul's day.

2.1.1.   Spears were anywhere from 5' long, all the way to the Macedonian lance of 24'.

2.1.2.   The Roman's spear that Paul was familiar with was called the *pilum*.

2.1.2.1.   They would hurl the *pilum* through the air, keeping the enemy from advancing close.

2.1.2.2.   The length of the *pilum* was 6', with an iron-pointed-head at the top and an iron shaft on the bottom. 7 feet of solid iron!

2.1.3.   It is also important to realize, there were many kinds and varieties of each spear.

2.1.3.1.   Various shapes
2.1.3.2.   Various sizes
2.1.3.3.   Various lengths

2.2. As he ends his metaphor on armor, Paul writes in Eph. 6:18. ⟶

2.2.1.   We will look closely at this verse, analyzing each phrase.

praying.......always

2.2.2.   The Greek word used here for "praying" includes thanksgiving, not just speaking, but also listening. It includes conversation and fellowship.

2.2.3.   The word "always" tells us to have an attitude of prayer at all times.

2.2.4.   Paul repeats the command to pray in 1 Thessalonians 5:17. ⟶

Ephesians 6:18 ....*praying always with all prayer and supplication in the Spirit, being watchful to this end with all perseverance and supplication for all the saints.* NKJV

pray without ceasing

2.2.5.   Prayer is something the Lord expects us to engage in constantly. This is possible because there are at least six different types of prayer. Consider: There is also an "attitude of prayer" which one may have at all times.

with all prayer

2.3. The literal Greek translation would be "*…..with all kinds of prayer.*"

NIV *And pray in the Spirit on all occasions with* <u>all kinds of prayers</u> *and requests.*

2.3.1.   There are many forms of prayer available for this air attack.

NASU <u>With all prayer and petition</u> *pray at all times in the Spirit…*

2.3.1.1.   For example there is a Prayer Dedication

DARBY *praying at all seasons, with* <u>all prayer and supplication</u> *in the Spirit.*

2.3.1.2.   Prayer of Petition

2.3.1.3.   Prayer of Faith and Authority

GOODSPEED <u>Use every kind of prayer.</u>

2.3.1.4.   Prayer of Praise and Worship

AMP *with all [manner of] prayer.*

2.3.1.5.   Prayer of Supplication

2.3.1.6.   Prayer of Thanksgiving

2.3.1.7.   and others I am sure.

2.3.2.   Paul instructs us to pick up and *use* each type of spear/prayer.

2.3.3.   Just as the Roman soldier had a short lance for thrusting at close range, and a long spear or lance to hurl a great distance, we have the prayer of faith filled with authority. If the enemy gets too close, faith is the mortal wound! If he tries a distant attack, hurl your prayer towards him, EVEN INTO THE DARKNESS.

2.3.3.1.   We can become efficient in every type of prayer, rendering the enemy's devices useless from striking our families, businesses, homes or churches and ministries.

2.3.3.2.   The same type of prayer will not be effective in all situations.

2.4. The message that Paul is driving home here in Ephesians is a message of compassion and care among the saints. He emphasizes.....   ⟶ *for all the saints*

---
in the Spirit

2.4.1.   However, praying with all types of prayer, is an impossible standard to achieve...until we add the phrase *"in the Spirit."*   ⟶ *....praying always with all prayer and supplication in the Spirit.*

2.4.2.   This is not a prayer of "thank you Lord for this food." Every believer is to allow the Holy Spirit (notice Spirit is correctly capitalized) to fill us and direct His will in every type of daily prayer.

---
watchful.......with all perseverance

2.5. Paul continues in Eph. 6 *watchful to this end with all perseverance and supplication*

2.5.1.   NASU *be on the alert with all perseverance*

2.5.2.   AMP *keep alert and watch with strong purpose and perseverance*

2.5.3.   NKJV *being watchful to this end with all perseverance*

Romans 8:26-27
So too the [Holy] Spirit comes to our aid and bears us up in our weakness; for we do not know what prayer to offer nor how to offer it worthily as we ought, but the Spirit Himself goes to meet our supplication and pleads in our behalf with unspeakable yearnings and groanings too deep for utterance 27 And He Who searches the hearts of men knows what is in the mind of the [Holy] Spirit [what His intent is], because the Spirit intercedes and pleads [before God] in behalf of the saints according to and in harmony with God's will. AMP

Word Depth

Watchful, meaning to "keep awake" or "sleepless." It expresses not a mere wakefulness, but rather the watchfulness of those who are intent upon a thing. Prayer is not lazy. Also found in Mk. 13:33 and Heb. 13:17.

Word Depth

Perseverance. A strong pursuit of a goal, never giving up. Literal meaning is "to be strong toward." Used in prayer and in the apostles' teaching. This exact word in Eph. 6, is the only time it is used.

Jude 20-21
But you, beloved, building yourselves up on your most holy faith, praying in the Holy Spirit,

2.6. **DISCUSS** and Consider six kinds of Prayer.

2.6.1.   **Dedication**, a prayer of consecration, such as the only time Jesus used the word "if" in prayer. Luke 22:42 *"Father, if it is Your will, take this cup away from Me; nevertheless not My will, but Yours, be done."* NKJV

2.6.1.1.   It is not a prayer to change something or receive something from God. Jesus did not change what He knew was God's will.

2.6.1.2.   This prayer knows what the Father wants me to do; I dedicate myself to that action.

2.6.1.3.   If we want to be available to do what Jesus wants us to do, only then can we pray "if it be your will."

2.6.1.4.   When ever Jesus prayed to change something, or to heal one, He did not say "if it be your will Father."

Group Activity. Find and note these six positions of prayer in the Bible:
1. Kneeling
2. Standing
3. Lifting up hands
4. Bowing
5. On One's face
6. Secrete prayer

2.6.2. **Petition**. This is a prayer to change things or receive something, a prayer of faith. A prayer for results. It can be a prayer of agreement with another believer. This is perhaps the prayer we use more than any other. A prayer which "asks."

Group Discussion
Read and discuss the following Scriptures:

2.6.2.1.   1 Sam. 1:12 *Now it came about, as she continued praying before the Lord.*

2.6.2.2.   1 Sam. 1:17-18 *and may the God of Israel grant your petition that you have asked of Him.*

2.6.2.3.   Acts 6:6 *And these they brought before the apostles; and after praying, they laid their hands on them.*

2.6.2.4.   James 5:16 *The effective prayer of a righteous man can accomplish much.* James 5:18 *Then he prayed again.*

2.6.2.5.   Jesus' prayer in John 11:41 was a prayer to change a situation. He did not pray "if it be your will." He knew the Word, had confidence it, and prayed it. *Father, I thank You that You have heard Me.*

2.6.2.6.   Realize that God owns all things, and can provide all things for you.

CLASS NOTES

Note: Be specific in this kind of prayer. God wants you to ask.

Matt. 18:19
Again I say to you, that if two of you agree on earth about anything that they may ask, it shall be done for them by My Father who is in heaven. This is not a might be done, it is a promised result. We are not to question; we use faith and trust and then wait.

God owns all things
Ps. 50:10-11
For every beast of the forest is Mine, The cattle on a thousand hills.
11 *"I know every bird of the mountains, And everything that moves in the field is Mine.*

Hag. 2:8-9
The *silver is Mine and the gold is Mine,'* declares the Lord of hosts.

Ps. 24:1
The earth is the Lord's, and all it contains.

Your petition to Him results in receiving what God owns.

2.6.3. **Faith and Authority.** An individual's prayer using faith. Jesus said this prayer can move mountains that are before you. Could also be used in agreement with another. It is a prayer with power (His power, not yours).

2.6.3.1. This prayer concerns spiritual, physical, and financial needs of believers. Jesus said in Mark 11:24 *Therefore I say to you, whatever <u>things</u> you ask when you pray, believe that you receive them, and you will have them.* NKJV

2.6.3.2. This is not a prayer of agreement with someone. It says *you ask*. Read it again. Mark 11:24 applies to <u>your</u> faith, <u>your</u> prayer.

2.6.3.3. It has to do with <u>natural things</u>, (*fig trees* and *mountains*). At other times Jesus prayed concerning a coin or loaf of bread. It also includes physical healing.

2.6.4. **Praise and Worship**. This is a prayer, which has nothing to do with receiving or even expecting to receive. Perhaps the most "impersonal" of all six types of prayers.

2.6.4.1. Read Acts 13:1-4. Notice there is no petition in their prayer. They ministered to the Lord.

2.6.4.2. Also notice it is a two way conversation. Verse 2 reads *the Holy Spirit said.* Expect to fellowship with Him in this prayer. Jesus said to *ask* the Father, even

---

CLASS NOTES

Matt. 21:21-22
*And Jesus answered and said to them, "Truly I say to you, if **you** have faith and **do not doubt**, **you** will not only do what was done to the fig tree, but even if **you say** to this mountain, 'Be taken up and cast into the sea,' it will happen. 22 "And all things **you ask** in prayer, believing, you will receive."*

3 John 2
Beloved, I pray that you may prosper in every way and [that your body] may keep well... AMP

though the Father knows of your needs. The reason is fellowship.

2.6.5. **Supplication**. Peter records *casting all your care upon Him, because He cares about you.* (1 Peter 5:7 from Holman Christian Standard Bible®).

→

2.6.5.1. This prayer "casts" your cares upon the Lord and commits problems to Him. This is the meaning of supplication or commitment.

2.6.5.2. Learn how to rest after you cast. Be at peace, knowing He takes your burden and carries it. It is no longer yours! Consider Heb. 4:1

2.6.6. **Intercession**. God looks for someone to intercede for specific needs. Especially pray that people will be saved.

2.6.6.1. *I searched for a man among them who would build up the wall and stand in the gap before Me for the land, so that I would not destroy it* Ezek. 22:30

2.6.6.2. Ps. 101:8 *Morning after morning I will root up all the wicked in the land, that I may eliminate all the evildoers from the city of the Lord.* AMP

CLASS NOTES

The AMP, perhaps captures this best, *Casting the whole of your care [all your anxieties, all your worries, all your concerns, once and for all] on Him, for He cares for you affectionately and cares about you watchfully.*

Heb 4:1
Therefore, let us fear if, while a promise remains of entering His rest, any one of you may seem to have come short of it.

Heb. 4:1 *Therefore we must be wary that, while the promise of entering his rest remains open, none of you may seem to have come short of it.* (NET Bible)

interceding in behalf of all the saints. AMP

supplication for all the saints. NKJV

A KEY THOUGHT FOR THIS WEEK

Reflect on the lessons concerning God's Armor and the Enemy's Weapons. Spiritually "put on" His armor. It takes daily action on your part, using prayer and faith. When you wear His armor, no problem or difficulty can defeat you. The enemy's weapons will be hurled towards you, but God's Armor is your protection. Have faith in that!

PARTICIPANT'S NOTES:

CLASS NOTES

END LESSON TWELVE/COURSE

www.ingramcontent.com/pod-product-compliance
Lightning Source LLC
Chambersburg PA
CBHW081544040426

42448CB00015B/3213